The
Malvern
Aviator

The
Malvern
Aviator
Richard Skinner

STACK
BOOKS

Smokestack Books
1 Lake Terrace, Grewelthorpe, Ripon HG4 3BU
e-mail: info@smokestack-books.co.uk
www.smokestack-books.co.uk

ISBN 9780995767584

Smokestack Books
is represented
by Inpress Ltd

Acknowledgements

Thanks are due to the editors of the following print and online publications in which these poems first appeared: *Amaryllis, Bare Fiction, Dark Matter 7, Elbow Room, The Fat Damsel, HARK, Haverthorn, The High Window, The Interpreter's House, Poetry Bay, Poetry Salzburg Review, Proletarian Poetry* and *Woven Tale*.

'The Cloud of Unknowing' was first published in the limited edition pamphlet *The Ecchoing Green: Poems Inspired by William Blake* (The Big Blake Project, 2015), with thanks to Rachel Searle.

'Fabiola' was commissioned to celebrate John Berger's ninetieth birthday and first published in Amarjit Chandan, Gareth Evans and Yasmin Gunaratnam (eds) *The Long White Thread of Words: Poems for John Berger* (Smokestack, 2016).

Big-ups and high fives to Jill Abram, Mona Arshi, Catherine Ayres, Jo Bell, Zelda Chappel, John Clegg, Jane Commane, Joey Connolly, Josephine Corcoran, Patrick Davidson Roberts, Josephine Dickinson, Ian Duhig, Robert Harper, Deborah Hobbs, Victoria Kennefick, Dan O'Brien, Autumn Richardson, Hilda Sheehan, Martha Sprackland, George Szirtes, Maria Taylor, Owen Vince, Andrew Wells & Tammy Yoseloff.

Special thanks to my 'poet brothers' Keith Hutson, Martin Malone, Roy Marshall & Peter Raynard.

Contents

'In the presence of extraordinary actuality,
consciousness takes the place of imagination.'
Wallace Stevens

The Cloud of Unknowing

There, it is done.
We have built squarely
in the dross of the land
a place of worship for our Lord.

It took years to sand the stone,
make flush the lines.
But, really, we were shaping our own
misshapen lives.

Scrape mud before you enter, be clean.
Embolden yourself – look up, look up!
The columns involve you,
all perpendicular, skyward.

The tracery, too, leads to heaven,
leavening the spirit.
The blue and red glass
stain your upturned face.

On the lectern, the text,
a pool of learning deeper
than all the sky, all the
windows of radiance.

Its great lesson is that,
when we are slain,
we walk through a door
and enter the *jardin*.

A wren and a hawk will
sit there in a wish tree,
and when you cry,
there will be no reply.

And the wren, not the hawk,
will fly to where none can climb
and will perch among the high rocks.
And a bell will sound.

Ardennes

A choir, beats, orbs of rain explode on the window.
Outside, the fields spread bleakly, the rivers are in spate,
blooming and ripening in their squalid courses. Larches

and spires are tracing paper in the general gloom.
Mounds are pregnant pauses. The long now
is stretched unbearably. The present shock runs

and runs along the rails. The invisible blur.
The urge to elucidate, explain, kills the moment
stone dead. What is left is wood, not trees,

only traces, hashtags. We are incapable of a lie,
yet there is no belief here, yet more leaves fall
blocking the way for those to come.

Bardo for Pablo

How can we make our days simpler?
Expect nothing. Prepare for the others to follow.

What should we aim for?
People don't change, they only stand more nakedly revealed.

So we're going backwards?
Yes, you become the person you should always have been.

What worries you most?
That now, in your days, suffering has come to take the place of prophets.

Where do the prophets go wrong?
Those who have 'belief' cling, but those who have faith let go.

How shall we know when it happens?
The elements coming together and all the channels clear.

Will I like what's waiting for me in the room?
You are already beyond the gravity of your mind's property.

Is it cold where you are?
You do not remember, but you were here once before.

If we take away all we know from who we are, what's left?
Everything you give away.

Corsican Ram's Skull

The two halves of the skull
stitched together like hems taken up.
Edges of eye sockets delicate frills
of milk teeth, an eel's tiny incisors.
Whirls of starburst nebulae deep
in the cochlear. Hairline cracks
run like river deltas across the blanched bone.
Horns like bark, growth lines a moraine
incrementally ascending a high col.
Nose and jaw bones, extended fronds,
gape open in a frozen baa.

Cinquain: Giacometti, 'Head/Skull' (1934)

Meta-
phor illumin-
ates the notion of sym-
ptom, metonymy sheds light on
desire.

Cento

Above, cumulous clouds stand like pillars of a temple, blades of light slicing down through the gaps. Gold has been born out of Nothingness, but they are a fabulous world filled with traps and snares. We are forbidden to fly over the oceans of cloud above mountains. I flick the throttle from time to time to keep up exactly 2100 revs. I run my eyes over the dials, checking the gauges, keeping balance by gyroscope, keeping each needle exactly where it should be. I look down at the sea, steaming in the rain like a great hot cauldron. Hollow or not, I can't land on it. The sea is part of a world that is not my world. Two hours of daylight left. I bank vertically and set my course for the sector between Alexandria and Cairo.

In normal life, men do not experience the passage of time. They live in a provisional stillness. From the clusters of light streaming wastefully away behind the glass, I can guess only dimly at the flow of the country, its villages, its enchanted domains of which I can grasp nothing, for I am a traveller. Little by little, I am giving up the sunlight. This death of the world takes place slowly. The earth rises and seems to spread like a mist. The earth and sky merge gradually. Little by little, I am abandoned by the light. The first stars tremble as if shimmering in green water. It will be a long time yet before they harden into diamonds. And still longer before I can witness the silent games of the shooting stars. I feel no fatigue, and it seems to me that I could fly on like this for ten years.

All the stars are out now, revolving slowly, a whole sky marking the hour. The moon is there, gleaming on the cold stone tiles of the sea, dipping towards the sands. I will receive no signal until I reach the Nile. Nothing interests me now but the glow of a narrow line of radium on the instrument screen. I reflect on my condition, lost in the desert and in danger, naked between sand and stars, distanced from the poles of my life by an excess of silence. I feel lost in interplanetary space, among a hundred inaccessible planets. I patrol solemnly between the Great Bear and Sagittarius and then tack towards Mercury.

Fabiola

for John Berger

A crimson veil and a paling face,
a figure straight out of a Book of Hours.
Moments of goodness are time machines
and beautiful eyes are telescopes to the unseen.

To see and the want to know are the same
– memory is just another way of knowing –
but I cannot recognise these three faces,
lowered, louvered and heavily modified.

Depth cannot be found in a single image,
but placed together, they move from space to time.
I have to look at many to see just one
and forever is space-bound, not found in time.

We only grasp things juxtaposed in clusters,
a mess of spilled materials, a cosmos.
A fuller grasp comes when all is brought to rest,
no longer fixed to the flux or the *durée*.

By setting the replica over the original,
what is lost is not time but the aura.
In the eyes of the creator, viewed *en masse*,
the true face is the stereoscopic view.

Found

There is a white sunrise.
We are dreaming of a shape within a blur
and the days are not full enough.
They come, they wake us,
and there I found myself more truly and more strange.

The Iris Gallery

To begin with, there is nothing, then
a deep nothing, then
there is a blue depth.

I pushed aside the blue curtain and
stepped into the Iris Gallery,
a cleared space, painted white and left empty.

At first, I didn't grasp it,
the work being asked of me with fire,
water and wind, live bodies,
the gold leaf and the spinning mandalas.
But then I understood and then
I was falling and there were other bodies falling, too,
leaping, like salmon.

Then I saw a woman lying naked in grass,
as though she had just made love.
She was holding a storm lantern that was still alight.
Her cheeks were coral pink
but her body was scorched –
burned by her flight, perhaps, or
maybe by the love in her heart.
The ground around her was scorched, too,
her body,
blue at the edges – an imprint, a
ghostly shadow.

A small silver spot arrived
in the corner of my eye,
a familiar emissary in its metallic livery
from the world of pain.
It grew into a ball of hot electricity, a
mass of writhing elvers.
In a split second, it triggered two jagged
cracks, splitting my point of
view into parapraxis.
Then the fizzing light spread across my
whole field of vision until I
could see nothing except
a great shoal of mackerel.

I was swimming now, my movement
a force-field through the water, which opposed me,
yet held me up, and I felt safe,
my blood in its element, pulsing
like eels slipping their way upstream,
against the current.

On cue, the silver fish were swimming with me,
little machines in the water,
and whatever turn I made, they made too,
enveloping me, escorting me
to a place as yet unfamiliar but that
will soon feel so close to home,
brighter and bluer than any
I have ever known.

Dark Nook

I am Egbert Clague.
I come every morning from Agneash
hoping for the nod from the bargain man.
It takes two hours to descend the ladders,
our tallow candles round our necks
like white asparagus.

The hole to go down is just two foot by two,
the spokes like blunt knives,
the blackdamp smelling awful. We chip
and hack until we see the sparkle
of the rich extraordinary,
haul it up through smoke to the adit.

One day, they brought me up
in the dead box, my leg crushed.
The Captain of the Mines
came in person to the cottage and said,
'We can't give you anything
and that will have to keep you.'

My wife Brenda is on the
Washing Floors now, sorting ore from stone
ready to ship to Swansea.
It's worse work than the mine—
she has no more feeling in her hands.
I'll be joining her there soon.

Meantime, I grow veg, read and
visit the village chapel on my sticks
to pray our Sooki will one day flee.
When I'm alone, I kneel and whisper,
*'The affection you get back from children
is sixpence as change from a sovereign.'*

The Summer of Red Mercedes

Your chestnut hair flared in the sun, an oil
spill in the ocean.

Beta-amyloids flushed our spines, a mass of
crill surfaced, pink-gold.

Legs pinned back like wings, our bodies systems of
pulleys and levers.

Your pubic bone lifted, a swan's head, and after, we
cleaved apart, like slate.

Black Water Side

Your mind is a house full of people running through rooms
looking for keys. Doors slam, but far away,
so softly you're not even sure you heard it. Turn
the door knob and step into the freezing landscape.
Notice the weeping willow bending over the beck.
The black water now runs red.

Your life is here, made up of minutes, hours, naps,
errands, routine. The little things have to be enough.
The valley is reduced to the side of a fell and cloud coming in.
The sheep are cragfast, the deer keep falling down.
You've nowhere else to go and you're sure of it now –
this is the wrong mountain.

Eclipse, Salisbury Plain, 1903

Standing by the Scots pine,
looking back at the house,
he knows he's been here before –
a slight flutter in his heart,
a panic in his throat,
when he sees the frosted windows
blind with unknowing cloud
looking at him indifferently.

His hands do their tremorous thing
as he winds up the contraption
and sets it off to the air.
All measures and weights calculated,
it is really his moonsick heart
that lifts and drifts to other skies.

Nightscape in grey/violet

12.55am. Pools of sodium light illuminate
corners of quiet streets. A neon blue
cross blazes from the Sally Army HQ.
The moon screened behind thin cloud, its centre
pale green, its aura tinged
orange, the whole sky
an Honorine Jobert anemone.
Moon-glow catches lead edges, metal
gutters – the waxy petals in the garden
spots of phosphoric white.

Via Fiori Oscuri

(Milan, 1 May 2015)

Flashes of cornices in puddles.
Street cleaners on tractor quads
that expel angry air from flues.

Pale striped awnings buffer on balconies,
a radio blares from a kiosk.
The Pinacoteca is closed.

A purple billboard announces
reticulated giraffes in the new zoo,
a recurrence of atavistic beasts.

Two cars smoulder near Bar Magenta,
anti-Expo graffiti on metal shutters,
the air perfumed with violence.

Later, a train to Bergamo Alta.
Factories like strips of magnesium,
barber pole stacks pumping effluence.

Up the funicular, amid the towers
the back alleys a nexus of admittance,
a confluence of ancient tongues.

Chinese Apples

In Kassel, my mother was told to buy three *Apfelsinen*.
Too shy an au pair to ask what that was,
she walked to the shop and asked
and was handed three oranges.
Back in the empty house, she went to bed.
She hadn't slept as the children
had planted an alarm clock in her wardrobe
set to go off at 3 a.m.
She was woken by the doorbell. It was
the father's brother come to visit.
He presented her with a single gladiola
which she must add to the vase
set in the mezzanine recess.
When she came down the stairs, he said,
'I am going to have an *Anfall*,'
stuffed a handkerchief in his mouth,
lay on the floor and had a fit.
She ran to the father's office next door
whereupon he hushed her
and stroked her knee while she sat
on the red leather chair.
Years later in Glasgow, my mother confessed.
She could never again eat oranges
without smelling gladioli or falling ill,
could never again sit still in churches.

The Astorians

My grandmother is sitting in a village hall
watching her Art play his sax.
She is 19 and is wondering when
they will have their first conjectural sex.

The hall is hot, too few windows open
that are far too high. Next to her, Bert
is too loud at his drums. Art's brother, Eric,
is dancing madly with a hussy named Kat.

My grandmother is waiting for the last song –
she has been here many times before –
when Art will unclip his instrument
to have the last dance with his Vera.

It is summer 1931, somewhere near Malvern Link,
well before the years of struggle with her
disabled daughter, the home
they eventually found for her in Worcester.

Then the War: the years of saving for furniture
because she didn't approve of HP.
Art's slow rise to Co-op Store Manager
in charge of women's outfits and drapery.

Later, she whispered to me how terrified
she was on her wedding night,
but how kind-hearted Art was,
who just hushed her and turned out the light.

In the home, she told me she fought every night
with the devil in her dreams.
Often, she would stare at me and demand to know
if she were standing in a stream.

But this is all still to come. Right now,
my grandmother looks at Art ('How handsome!'),
notices the shine of his bow tie and single button,
the big A on the kick drum.

The Malvern Aviator

for Richie McCaffery

My father's watch. One of only a few hundred.
Dark blue face, Arabic numerals.
It keeps terrible time. I wear it now
only to counterweigh the days,
the equinoxes and leap years.

When there is an odd jump in time
(the clocks going forward),
it even-keels me, like bike stabilisers,
swimming wings.
I do not fall down, I do not drown.

But if I were to take it off and abandon it
by my large granite basin,
its hands would fail with the iron
and I would venture out in the world,
ending up as a heap of ashes.

Notes

'The Cloud of Unknowing' is an anonymous work of Christian mysticism written in the late 14th century that inspired The Lollards, a Protestant sect who rose to prominence across the south of England during the reign of Richard II.

The source material for 'Cento' is *Wind, Sand and Stars* by Antoine de Saint-Exupéry.

'Fabiola' refers to an installation of over 300 portraits of a fourth-century Christian saint collected by the artist Francis Alÿs. In all of these portraits, Fabiola is depicted in profile with her head covered in a rich red veil.

The source material for 'Found' is Lotte Kramer, Ian Hamilton, Ezra Pound, Philip Larkin & Wallace Stevens.

'Dark Nook' was written after a visit to the old Laxey mine with its Great Wheel on the Isle of Man.